DAY TRADING OPTIONS

Copy Strategies, Volatility in the Market, COVID-19
Will Affect Option Trading

Robert Vandusen

TABLE OF CONTENTS

Introduction 5
Chapter 1: Day Trading 11
    What Is Day Trading? 11
    Dos of Day TradingRisk Capital 12
    Research 13
    Diversification 13
    Stop Loss 14
    Take a Loss 14
    Don'ts of Day TradingNo Planning 15
    Over Rely on Broker 15
    Message Boards 16
    Calculate Wrong 16
    Copy Strategies 17
Chapter 2.   Volatility in the Market 18
    Historical Volatility 18
    Implied Volatility 18
    The Impact of Volatility on Options Trades 19
    How to Compute Historical Volatility 21
    How to Compute Implied Volatility 22
Chapter 3.   Typical Beginners Mistakes inOptions 24
    Ignoring the Statistics Behind Options Trading 25
    Not Being Adaptable 26
    Ignoring the Probability 28
    Not Considering Exotic Options 29
    Not Keeping Earnings and Dividend Dates in Mind 31
Chapter 4. Important Trading Principles to Follow 33
    Ensure Good Money Management 33

Ensure That Risks and Rewards Are Balanced 35
Develop a Consistent Monthly Options Trading System 36
Consider a Brokerage Firm That is Right for Your Level of
Options Expertise 37
Broker Services and Features 38
Commissions and Other Fees 39
Ensure That Exits are automated 41

Chapter 5.   Buy an Equity at a Lower Price 42
Trading Beams with Large Margins 42
Purchase Zones 43
The Stop 45
Profit Taking 46
Anticipation 47
The Time-Break-Out Rule 48
Price Gaps 49

Chapter 6. Options Pricing 52
Strike Price and Underlying Price 53
Factors That Affect an Option's Price 55
History of the Black-Scholes Model 56
Stock Price 57
Strike Price 57
Type of Option 58
Time to expiration 59
Interest Rates 59
Dividends 61
Volatility 61

Chapter 7.   Tips and Tricks in Stocks 63
The Price of Any Stock Can Move in 3 Basic Directions 63
Before Buying a Call or Put Option, Look at the Underlying
Stock's Chart 65
Chart Readings and Buying Call Options 66

    Chart Readings and Buying Put Options 66
    Chart Readings for Purchase of Call and Put Options 67
    Find Out the Breakeven Point Before Buying Your Options 67
    Calculating the Breakeven Point 68
    If You Are Dealing with Call and Put Options, Embrace the Underlying Stock's Trend 68
    When Trading Options, Watch Out for Earnings Release Dates .. 69

Chapter 8.   How to Double or Triple Your Returns 71
    Buy Low and Sell High 72
    Focus on Not Losing Money Rather Than on Making Money 73
    Develop a Sense of Sentiment Analysis 74
    Learn from Your Competitors 77
    Cash-Out 78
    Take a Break and Have Fun 79

Chapter 9. How to Become a Millionaire with Option Trading 81
    Writing Options 81
    The Straddle Strategy 82
    The Collar Strategy 83
    The Strangle Strategy 83
    Options Trading is Quite Profitable 84
    The Most Profitable Options Trading Strategy 85
    Consistently Profitable Strategies – Selling Puts & Credit Spreads 87
    Overall Best Options Trading Strategy 87
    A Closer Look at Naked Puts 89
    ROI or Return on Investment 90

Chapter 10. How COVID-19 Will Affect Option Trading 92
    Equity Trading is Also on the Rise 97

Conclusion 100

Introduction

It is near impossible to predict market movements, and that is why day traders, swing traders, and forex traders place trades of any length in which they take a position with the hope that the price will move favorably for them. Day trading, swing trading, and forex trading can all be profitable in the long term if done correctly. Give one or more of these strategies a try!

Day Trading

Day trading involves making short-term trades on assets such as stocks or currencies with the goal of making a quick profit when you buy an assetand sell it at a higher price before its value decreases. To do this, day tradersgenerally enter a position and then exit it if the price does not move in their favor. In the long term, day trading can be profitable for traders who know what to do to make correct trades at optimal times and avoid losing money due to falls in the stock market. Day trading can be very high risk, and taking excessive risks can lead to devastating losses over time.

Swing Trading

Swing trading involves taking a position in an asset over a longer period of time (ranging from days to years). When a swing trader first enters a trade, it is called a long position because they will be holding the asset for some time. If the price does not go up or down in their favor, they will be happy with their profit or loss. But if the price increases significantly by the end of the time frame, then they are considering taking an opposite position by selling the shares or contracts at that point. This strategy takes more effort and can take more than one year to make money, but it also has less risk than day trading.

Forex Trading

Forex trading involves buying and selling currencies. The market is open 24 hours a day, so it is possible to trade on the short-term fluctuations in the market. Just as with stocks, currencies can be more volatile than others at times. A successful forex trader should be able to identify trends, determine their risk tolerance and time frame for trades, manage risks accordingly, and be able to stick with a plan through thick and thin.

Day Trading VS. Forex Trading VS. Swing Trading

Before I go any further, let me define what these terms mean. The most basic concept is that they refer to the same groups of conditions. But to be clear, Forex involves currency trading; day trading involves the buying and selling of stocks or futures; swing trading involves both stocks and futures.

The average Forex trade takes about 40-60 days to make money on a short- term basis (2-4 weeks). It might take even longer if the market is moving too fast or if it's in a tight range for too long. A long-term trend will generally move at a faster pace than short-term trends.

If you are going to day trade, then I recommend day trading the trend. Always trade what the trend is doing. I can make more money on a trend than on a range, and while I was trading in one of my previous blogs, I hada 15-year streak of daily winning trades where my little brother could not beat me. I made money. It might be different in your account but it makes sense that the following something works better than trying to anticipateand trade against it (when you should never do that).

Swing trading is in between and generally involving very few trades. I've noticed that swing trading sometimes takes a longer time than day trading due to the fact that you are not looking for explosive moves up or down, but a slow gradual move. But it can be done much quicker than forex if the market is volatile, so keep that in mind.

Here's where trend following comes in. Momentum begets moremomentum, while range-bound markets are very hard to trade in the short term because there's nowhere to go but up or down when the range is too small.

Day trading is a versatile strategy that can be used to earn a profit without taking any risk. For example, traders can buy a stock and hold it for severalweeks to months in order to collect dividends or sell short.

Swing traders are generally more risk-averse than day traders because they are not trying to capture small gains; instead, they aim at higher profits overlonger time periods. Investors who are willing to take the time to learn howto swing trade from the start will likely be rewarded in the long term.

What You Will Discover in This Book

I am a straightforward guy, so you will find that I like to get right to the point. There will be no beating around the bush. I will not spout out terms atyou like this is a textbook. All the words in this book are meant to be understood by a complete newbie.

Before we get to these explanations, one thing needs to be stated: day trading is a business. I will remind you that throughout this book, it's suchan important thing to understand. Companies do not just spring up and become successful overnight, even though it sometimes appears that way tooutsiders. Businesses take hours of devotion every day and months of behind-the-curtain work to become successful. In the case of day trading, it usually takes between 3 and 6 months of regular time and effort to get your feet firmly planted on the ground to see the results you want.

Trading is not a get-rich-quick scheme. If you do not have the time it takes to learn the business's ins and outs, this is not your career. In fact, you must commit the right amount of time, be able to handle a challenge or the excitement of an ever-changing career, and have the will to learn and grow.

It is possible to make money through all three of these strategies, but ittakes practice and knowledge. If you like the idea of any of these three methods, it is important that you practice your trading strategy and learn more about technical analysis. Technical analysis involves examining past price behavior to predict future price movement.

With some determination and a lot of effort, you can be a successful trader in any of these fields.

This book will discuss these three strategies, and how they are related toone another.

Are you ready to be serious about gaining new tools and skills that will allow you to take control of your financial future? If so, then read on! I promise that this book will let you hit the ground running with day trading, even though you are starting with zero knowledge and experience.

Don't wait and miss out on the opportunity to take control of your finances and your life. Procrastination will keep you chained to financial slavery. Read this book in its entirety to see how YOU can be the master of your destiny!

We have a lot of ground to cover in a few pages. So, let's get started.

Chapter 1: Day Trading

What Is Day Trading?

The stock market is a vast place and there are millions of trades that take place all over the world, within a single day. There are both buyers and sellers in the market, and they will all have the same motive in mind; to increase their wealth potential.

Of all these trades, not everything will be of the same nature. Some will be long-term investments and some short. Long-term investments refer to those that are held for a long period of time. They are preferred by those who are not in a hurry to make money. Short-term investments, on the otherhand, are those that are liquidated within a short period of time. They arenot intended to be held for a long time, as owners will be interested in disposing of them early.

Short-term investments can be of many types based on the time that they are held. Some can be held for a month, some for a week, and some will be disposed of on the same day. This book will focus on the last option.

Better known as Intraday trading, day trading is one of the most preferred ways to trade in the stock market. Preferred mostly by those willing to part with their investment within a single day and realize a profit, or loss, from.

Intraday traders are interested in realizing a profit by capitalizing on the difference in the rates of these securities as opposed to long-term investors who will be in it for the Dividends.

Dos of Day Trading Risk Capital

You have to understand that the stock market is a very volatile place, and anything can happen within a matter of a few seconds. You have to be prepared for anything that it throws at you. In order to prepare for it, you have to make use of risk capital. Risk capital refers to money that you are willing to risk. You have to convince yourself that even if you lose the money that you have invested, then it will not be a big deal for you. For that, you have to make use of your own money and not borrow from anyone, as you will start feeling guilty about investing it. Decide on a set number and invest it.

Research

Before you invest in the market, you need to research it thoroughly. Don't think you're going to learn as you go along. That is only possible if you at least know the basics. You have to remain interested in gathering information that is crucial for your investments, and it will only come about if you put in some hard work towards it. Nobody is asking you to stay up and go through thick texts books. All you have to do is go through books and websites and gather enough information to help you get started on the right foot.

Diversification

You have to stress diversification in your portfolio. You don't want all the money to go into the same place. Think of it as a way to increase your stock's potential. You have to choose different sectors and diverse stocks to invest in. you should also choose one of the different types of investments as they all contribute towards attaining a different result. Diversification is mostly seen as a tool to cut down on risk, and it is best that you not invest any more than 5% in any one of the securities.

Stop Loss

You have to understand the importance of a stop-loss mechanism. A stop- loss technique is used to safeguard an investment. Now say, for example, you invest $100 and buy shares priced at $5 each. You have to place a stop loss at around $4 in order to stop it from going down any further. Now you will wonder as to why you have to place the stop loss and undergo one. Well, by doing so, you will actually be saving your money to a large extent. You won't have to worry about the value slipping further down and can carry on with your trade.

Take a Loss

It's okay to have losses from time to time. Don't think of it as a big obstacle. You will have the opportunity to turn a loss into profit. You have to remain confident and invested. You can take a loss on a bad investment that was anyway not going your way. You can also take a loss on an investment that you think is a long hold and will not work for you in the short term. Taking a few losses is the only way in which you can learn to trade well in the market.

These form the different dos of the stock market that will help you with your intraday trades.

Don'ts of Day Trading No Planning

Do not make the mistake of going about investing in the market without a plan in tow. You have to plan out the different things that you will do in the market and go about it the right way. This plan should include how much you will invest in the market, where you will invest, how you will go about it etc. No planning will translate to getting lost in the stock market, which is not a good sign for any investor.

Over Rely on Broker

You must never over rely on a broker. You have to make your own decisions and know what to do and when. The broker will not know whether an investment is good for you. He will only be bothered about his profits. If he is suggesting something, then you should do your own research before investing in the stock. The same extends to emails that you might receive through certain sources. These emails are spams and meant to dupe you. So, don't make the mistake of trusting everything that you read.

Message Boards

You have to not care about message boards. These will be available on the Internet and are mostly meant to help people gather information. But there will be pumpers and bashers present there. Pumpers will force people to buy a stock just to increase its value, and bashers will force people to sell all their stocks just because they want the value to go down. Both these types are risky, as they will abandon the investors just as soon as their motive is fulfilled. So, you have to be quite careful with it.

Calculate Wrong

Some people make the mistake of calculating wrong. They will not be adept at math and will end up with wrong figures. This is a potential danger to all those looking to increase their wealth potential. If you are not good at calculating, then download n app that will do it for you or carry a calculator around to do the correct calculations. The motive is to make the right calculations and increase your wealth potential.

Copy Strategies

Do not make the mistake of copying someone else's strategies. You have to come up with something that is your own and not borrowed from someone else. If you end up borrowing, then you will not be able to attain the desired results. You have to sit with your broker and come up with a custom strategy that you can employ and win big.

These form the different don'ts of the stock market that will help you keep troubles at bay.

Chapter 2. Volatility in the Market

We can define volatility as a statistical measure of the levels of fluctuations of stock, shares, or the entire market. The value is calculated as the ASD or annualized standard deviation of the price swings of security in terms of daily percentage. The value is expressed as a percentage.

Historical Volatility

Historical volatility is simply a measure of a security's volatility in the past. When computing this figure, you will have to define a specific period for consideration. One of the most common figures used for historical volatility is 20 days. This specific measure approximates total trading day numbers within a month.

Implied Volatility

Another useful term is implied volatility. This measures the volatility that is implied by the prevailing market price of the stock's options. Implied volatility is computed using one of the main option pricing models, like the Black Scholes Model. Using this or similar models, you can work out volatility where a mathematical relationship has been established relating to the price of an option and the volatility of the underlying stock.

Implied volatility provides insights into the market's view of the options contracts' underlying security. It can be determined by making use of the following:

Option's current market price

The value of the underlying security Expiration dates

The strike prices

Any applicable interest rates Any applicable dividend yields

In an ideal situation, we would expect the implied volatility figure to be the same for all options that have the same expiry date. This is regardless of the strike price that was used in our computations. In practice, however, this is hardly accurate because the figures we get vary mostly due to strike prices. This variation in volatility is known as the volatility skew.

The Impact of Volatility on Options Trades

We have already established what the term volatility means in options trading. It is simply a measure of the size and rate of the price change of the underlying security. High volatility implies a high option premium. The reverse is also true.

If you can accurately assess the value of statistical volatility for the underlying security, you will be able to use this value in a pricing model for purposes of computing a fair market price for the option. It is crucial that, as an options trader, you keep in mind the fact that changes in volatility can greatly impact your trades either negatively or positively.

Historical volatility generally measures the speed at which a futures commodity or stock price has moved in the past. This enables you to predict with some degree of accuracy, its expected movement in the future.

For instance, if we have a vehicle that is traveling at 50 miles per hour, we can determine how many miles it will travel for the entire year.

Distance = speed * time

In our case, distance = 50 mph * 24 hours/day * 365 days/year = 438,000km

If everything remains constant, then we can accurately predict the distance that the car will cover. However, in real life, this is hardly the case because the car could make stops, break down sometimes, and so on. The same is true for stocks and options. Although our calculations depend on known factors, if the variables keep changing, the outcome could be different.

How to Compute Historical Volatility

Historical volatility is quantifiable and is based largely on previous changes to a futures or stock options contract. To calculate this figure, you need to consider the past prices and all price changes, then average them out into a percentage.

For instance, you can consider the historical volatility for 10 days. If you have the price change for 10 days in percentage terms, you should subtract the daily percentage price variations to find deviations from the average daily change for the period.

One of the most common methods that can be used to compute historical volatility is the close-to-close changes in percentage for daily values. There is another method known as the high minus low prices. Another approach would be to take an average of low, high, and median prices. The purpose of all these models is to obtain some intraday information that is usually notincluded in a close-to-close system.

It is also advisable to spend a few moments calculating historical volatility as well as the trending vs. trading range markets. A stable trend will likely emerge, and it can go either up or down but will not affect the size of percentage price changes.

While the changes in average daily price may increase, historical volatility as calculated may become smaller. Also, it is possible to demonstrate that historical volatility figures can increase if the average daily price reduces in size regardless of the market trends. One of the most popular methods uses 10 days of daily percentage price changes. This information is then used also to compute a standard deviation. Commonly used are 20 and 30 days and specific time frames for your computations.

How to Compute Implied Volatility

It is a lot easier to look at implied volatility with common pricing models such as the Black-Scholes model. You will need to have at least five inputs or variables.

With these inputs, you will receive a more accurate and reliable theoretical option price. However, most of the time, the markets do not set the fair value price for the same option. Options prices will normally deviate from these theoretical values. The fair price is a result of the input of five independent variables.

In general, if the market price exceeds the theoretical price of an option, then market participants such as traders and investors have added a premium to the price. A lot of these concepts are best viewed with real-life examples.

Commodity options usually portray excellent volatility. When the markets portray high volatility, then traders should be careful of buying options straight up. It would be a lot better to sell than to buy at this point. When the volatility is low, then options buyers should start buying.

Chapter 3. Typical Beginners Mistakes in Options

"Well, now we know what not to do."

Inexperienced traders are often warned away from purchasing options that are out of the money as being a greater risk than the ultimate reward is likely to be. While it is true that a short expiration time coupled with an out of the money option will frequently look appealing, especially to those with a smaller amount of trading capital to work with, the issue is that all of these types of options are likely to look equally appealing which leaves them with no way to tell the good from the bad.

As a more experienced trader, however, you have many more tools at your disposal than the average novice which means that, while risky, cheap options have the potential to generate substantial returns, as long as you keep the following in mind while trading them.

Ignoring the Statistics Behind Options Trading

One of the biggest mistakes that most newbie options traders make is that they forget the probability is a real thing. When you check a potential stock before purchasing an option, it's important to understand that the history of an option is important when deciding whether or not you should be investing in it, but so are the odds and probability surrounding whether or not a particular event is going to occur.

For example, a common strategy that investors use is to leverage their money by investing in cheap options so that this will help to prevent big losses on a stock that they actually own shares of. Of course, this is a good strategy, but nothing works one-hundred percent of the time. Make sure that if the rules of probability and simple ratios are telling you to stay away from a deal, you listen to the facts staring you in the face. Wishful thinking will come to bite you later on.

Being overzealous: Frequently, when new options traders finally get their initial plan just right, they become overzealous and start committing to larger trades than they can realistically afford to recover from if things go poorly. It is important to take it slow when it comes to building your rate ofreturn and never bet more than you can afford to lose.

Regardless of how promising a specific trade might seem, there is no risk/reward level at which it is worth considering a loss that will take you out of the game completely for an extended period of time. Trade reasonably and trade regularly and you will see greater results in the long-term guaranteed.

Not Being Adaptable

The successful options trades know when to follow their plans but they alsoknow that no plan will be the right choice, even if early indicators say otherwise. There is a difference between making a point of sticking to a plan and following it blindly and knowing which is one of the more important indicators of the separation between options trading success and abject failure. This means it is important to be aware of when and where experimentation and new ideas are appropriate and when it is best to toe the line and gather more data in order to make a well-reasoned decision.

This also means having several different plans in your options trading toolbox and not just resolutely sticking to the first one that brings you a modicum of success. This is crucial as there are certain plans that will only work in specific situations and knowing which to use when, in real-time, will lead to significantly greater returns on a more reliable basis every single time.

Likewise, an adaptive options trader knows that market conditions can change unexpectedly and is prepared to respond accordingly. This means understanding when the time is right to go in a new direction, regardless of the potential risks that doing so might entail.

Sometimes a good trader has to make a leap of faith, and a trader who is successful in the long term knows what signs to look for that indicate this type of scenario is occurring in real-time. Unfortunately, this type of foresight cannot be taught and instead must be found with experience.

As long as you keep the appropriate mindset regarding individual trades, any new strategy that is attempted will result in valuable data, if nothing else. It is important to understand that learning not to use a specific course of action a second time is always valuable, no matter the costs. Working to build this into your core trading mindset will lead you to greater success in a wider variety of situations in the long term.

Ignoring the Probability

Always remember that the historical data will not apply to the current trends in the market at all times which means you will always want to consider the probability as well as the odds that the market is going to behave the way it typically does. The odds are how likely the market is to behave as expected and the probability is the ratio of the likelihood of a given outcome. Understanding the probability of certain outcomes can make it easy to purchase the proper options to minimize losses related to holdings of specific underlying stocks.

When purchasing cheap options, it is important to remember that they are always going to be cheap for a reason as the price is determined by the strike price of the underlying stock as well as the amount of time remaining for the option to regain its value, choose wisely otherwise you are doing little more than gambling and there are certainly better ways to gamble than via options trading.

Not Considering Exotic Options

An exotic option is one that has a basic structure that differs from either European or American options when it comes to the how and when of how the payout will be provided or how the option relates to the underlying asset in question.

Additionally, the number of potential underlying assets is going to be much more varied and can include things like what the weather is like or how much rainfall a given area has experienced. Due to the customization options and the complexity of exotic options, they are only traded over the counter.

While they are undoubtedly more complex to get involved with, exotic options also offer up several additional advantages when compared to common options, including:

- They are a better choice for those with very specific needs when it comes to risk management.
- They offer up a variety of unique risk dimensions when it comes to both management and trading.
- They offer a far larger range of potential investments that can more easily meet a diverse number of portfolio needs.
- They are often cheaper than traditional options.

They also have additional drawbacks, the biggest of which is that they cannot often be priced correctly using standard pricing formulas. This may work as a profit instead of a drawback, however, depending on if the mispricing falls in favor of the trader or the writer.

It is also important to keep in mind that the amount of risk that is taken on with exotic options is always going to be greater than with other options due to the limited liquidity each type of exotic option is going to have available.

While some types are going to have markets that are fairly active, others are only going to have limited interest. Some are even what are known as dual-party transactions which means they have no underlying liquidity and are only traded when two amiable traders can be found.

Not Keeping Earnings and Dividend Dates in Mind

It is important to keep an eye on any underlying assets that you are currently working with as those who are currently holding calls have the potential to be assigned early dividends, with greater dividends having an increased chance of this occurrence.

As owning an option doesn't mean owning the underlying asset, if this happens to you, then you won't be able to collect on your hard-earned money. The early assignment is largely a random occurrence which means if you don't keep your ear to the ground, it can be easy to get caught unaware and be unable to exercise the option before you miss the boat.

Along similar lines, you are going to also always want to be aware of when the earnings season is going to take place for any of your underlying assets as it is likely going to increase the price of all of the contracts related to the underlying asset in question.

Additionally, you will need to be caught up on current events as even the threat of influential news can be enough to cause a significant spike in volatility and premiums as well. In order to minimize the additional costsassociated with trading during these periods, you are going to want to utilize a spread. Doing so will minimize the effect inflation has on your bottom line.

Chapter 4. Important Trading Principles to Follow

You need to take it a step further by applying principles that will reinforce that plan. Think of that trading plan as the foundation of your house of success. The policies below are the bricks to develop your home into what you want it to be.

Ensure Good Money Management

Money is the tool that keeps the engine of the financial industry performing in good working order. You must learn to manage your money in a way that works for you instead of against you as an options day trader. It is an intricate part of maintaining your risk and increasing your profit.

Money management is the process whereby monies are allocated for spending, budgeting, saving, investing, and other procedures. Money management is a term that any person with a career in the financial industry, and particularly in the options trading industry, is intimately familiar with because this allocation of funds is the difference between a winning options trader and a struggling options trader.

Below you will find tips for managing your money so that you have maximum control of your options day trading career.

Money Management Tips for Options Traders

Define money goals for the short term and the long term so that you can envision what you would like to save, invest, etc. Ensure that these are recorded and easily accessed. Your trading plan will help you define your money goals.

Develop an accounting system. There is a wide range of software that can help with this, but it does not matter which one you use if you can establish records and efficiently track the flow of your money.

Use position sizing to manage your money. Position sizing is the process of determining how much money will allocate to entering an options position. To do this effectively, allocate a smart percentage of your investment fund toward individual options. For example, it would be unwise to use 50% of your investment fund on one option. That is 50% of your capital that can potentially go down the drain if you make a loss in that position. A good percentage is using no more than 10% of your investment fund toward individual option positions. This percentage allocation will help you get through tough periods, which eventually happen without having all your funds lost.

Never, ever invest money that you cannot afford to lose. Do not let emotion override this principle and cloud your judgment.

Spread your risks by diversifying your portfolio. You expand your portfolio by spreading your wealth by investing in different areas, add to your investments regularly, being aware of commissions always, and knowing when to close a position.

Develop the day trading styles and strategies that earn you a steady rate of return. Even if you use scalping where the returns are comparatively small, that constant flow of profit can add up big over time.

Ensure That Risks and Rewards Are Balanced

To ensure that losses are kept to a minimum and that returns are as high as they can be, options day traders should use the risk/reward ratio to determine each and to make adjustments as necessary. The risk/reward ratio is an assessment used to show profit potential concerning potential losses. It requires knowing the potential risks and profits associated with an options trade. Potential risks manage by using a stop-loss order. A stop-loss order is a command that allows you to exit a position in an options trade once a certain price threshold has reached.

Profit targeted using an established plan. Potential profit calculates by finding the difference between the entry price and the target profit. It is calculated by dividing the expected return on the options investment by the standard deviation.

Another way to manage risks and rewards is by diversifying your portfolio. Always spread your money across different assets, financial sectors, and geographies. Ensure that these different facets of your portfolio are not closely related to each other so that if one goes down, they don't all fall. Be smart about protecting and building your wealth.

Develop a Consistent Monthly Options Trading System

The aim of doing options trading is to have an overall winning options trading month. That will not happen if you trade options here and there. You cannot expect to see a huge profit at the end of the month if you only performed 2 or 3 transactions.

You need to have a high options trading frequency to up the chances of coming out winning every month. The only way to do that is to develop a sytem where you perform options trades at least five days a week.

Consider a Brokerage Firm That is Right for Your Level of Options Expertise

There are four essential factors that you need to consider when choosing a broker, and they are:

The requirements for opening a cash and margin account.

The unique services and features that the broker offers. The commission fees and other fees charged by the broker. The reputation and level of options expertise of the broker.

Look at these individual components to see how you can use them to power up your options day trading experience.

Broker Cash and Margin Accounts

Every options trader needs to open a cash account and margin account to be able to perform transactions. They are simply tools of the trade. A cash account is one that allows an options day trader to perform operations via being loaded with cash. Margin account facilitates transactions by allowing that to borrow money against the value of security in his or their account.

Both types of accounts require that a minimum amount deposited. It can beas few as a few thousand dollars to tens of thousands of dollars depending on the broker of choice. You need to be aware of the requirements when deliberating which brokerage firm is right for you.

Broker Services and Features

There are different types of services and features available from various brokerage firms. For example, if an options trader would like to have an individual broker assigned to him or her to handle his or her account personally, then he or she will have to look for a full-service broker. In thisinstance, there minimum account requirements that need to meet. Also, commission fees and other fees are generally higher with these types of brokerage firms. While the prices are higher, this might be better for a beginner trader to have that full service dedicated to their needs and the learning curve.

On the other hand, if an options trader does not have the capital needed to meet the minimum requirements of a full-service broker or would prefer tobe more in charge of his or her option trades, then there is the choice of going with a discount brokerage firm. The advantage to discount brokerage firms is that they tend to have lower commissions and fees. Most internet brokerage firms are discount brokers.

Other features that you need to consider when choosing a brokerage firm include:

Whether or not the broker streams real-time quotes.

The speed of execution for claims.

The availability of bank wire services. The availability of monthly statements.

How confirmations achieve, whether written or electronic.

Commissions and Other Fees

Commission fees paid when an options trader enters and exits positions. Every brokerage firm has its commission fees set up. These typically developed around the level of account activity and account size of the options trader.

These are not the only fees that an option trader needs to consider when considering brokerage firms. Many brokerage firms charge penalty fees for withdrawing funds and not maintaining minimum account balances — the existence of costs such as these cuts on options trader's profit margin.

Payment of fees needs to be kept to a minimum to gain maximum income, and as such, an options trader needs to be aware of all charges that exist and how they are applied when operating with a brokerage firm. It needs to be done before signing up.

Reputation and Options Expertise

You do not want to be scammed out of your money because you chose the wrong brokerage firm. Therefore, you must choose a broker that has an established and long-standing reputation for trading options. You also want to deal with a brokerage firm that has excellent customer service, that can aid in laying the groundwork for negotiating reduced commissions and allows for flexibility.

Ensure That Exits are automated

Even though I have stated that emotions should set aside when trading options, we are all human, and emotions are bound to come into the equation at some point. Knowing this is imperative that systems develop to minimize the impact of emotions. Having your exits automated is one such step that you can take to ensure that emotions are left out when dealing with options day trading. Using bracket orders facilitates this.

A bracket order is an instruction given when an options trader enters a new position that specifies a target or exit and a stop-loss order that aligns with that. This order ensures that a system is set up to record two points — the goal for-profit and the maximum loss point that will tolerate before the stop-loss comes into effect. The execution of either order cancels the other.

Chapter 5. Buy an Equity at a Lower Price

$$\frac{30 \text{ Owned Shares}}{100 \text{ Total Shares}} = 30\% \text{ Equity Stake}$$

$$\frac{30 \text{ Owned Shares}}{150 \text{ Total Shares}} = 20\% \text{ Equity Stake}$$

Low margins can be very useful when trading. To use them successfully, they must be integrated into the overall pattern. The basic idea is to enter the market as soon as it breaks out of the state of equilibrium that exists. If the price rises sharply from this point on and then falls back down there, an increase in demand is expected. This is a classic double bottom. In combination with the Accumulation / Distribution, this becomes the basis for an interesting trading approach. Choose only the trades in the direction of the thrust. Place stops at the opposite end of the short bar.

Trading Beams with Large Margins

A wide-span bar can be either bullish or bearish, depending on where it appears in the formation. If it appears at the end of a buy peak, then it is to be classified as bearish, at the break from a formation, however positive.

Most beams with a large span are followed directly by a correction beam. The buy zone is in the lower half of the bar, and the profit-taking area is located at around 50% to 100% of the span above the high of the bar. Of course, this only applies to short-term traders. The course tends to be varied, with a short track following a long bar. Of course, this is not always the case, and the definition of a wide-span bar is subjective. This is where the art of chart reading comes into play. This ability can only be learned by analyzing many charts over the years.

Purchase Zones

The buy zone describes the lower half of a push. While the relapses are causing the price to rise, the buying zone also moves upwards. In these areas, you should look for opportunities to get started. Before you open your position, you should know where to set the stop and set a price target. Mark the buy zone, the stop loss, and the area of the price target in the chart. Do not chase after a quick course! Among the countless stocks, there is always a good candidate for a better start. Opt for a boarding area. The following steps could help:

Buy only in the purchase zones.

Place your stop loss immediately after opening your position.

Be sure to close the position when you reach the winning zone. Is this done by means of a stop, or are you simply selling? Any possibility is a compromise: if you sell, the price could rise even higher. Waiting for the stop to be triggered will often result in significant portions of the potential win.

The following options are available:

Make the stop tighter.

Close only half the position. So, your decision is only half wrong or half correct.

Close your position at the first sign that the supply outweighs the demand.

Use a shorter time frame to set the stop. For example, if you trade on a daily chart, choose a 30-minute chart to place your stop more accurately.

The Stop

If you do not know what you are risking, you risk everything. There is no stop-loss option that is equally satisfactory for everyone. Everyone has to find out for himself which ratio of risk to the potential profit he feels comfortable with. Here are some suggestions for placing stop orders:

Three ticks below the low of the last or penultimate fulcrum

An average range below the closing price or the low of the day on which the purchase was made

50% of the breakout or break-in after opening the day after entering the position. This stop works especially well when combined with the other possible stops. For example, a value sometimes opens below a stop at a level, which then turns out to be the low of the day. We like to see it move about eight ticks or half the span of the previous bar after opening.

Three ticks below the lower low or lower end of the last two bars Close the position after three bars, if it is not yet in the profit zone.

Release the trade and try to exit without loss if the trade runs too far against you after the opening and your stop is not triggered. Do not think about a possible profit anymore. Their only interest is the stopping and preservation of your capital.

It is of utmost importance to always have a good plan ready for your investment. When opening a position, ask yourself if this is a long-term investment for five or ten years or not. Then you should not panic in the face of short-term price fluctuations. Are you a trader? Unfortunately, many people set their exit point or stop loss according to the following criteria:

The stop-loss is at a point where the losses are already huge.

The stop is based on the general market situation. If the whole market collapses, my positions will be closed.

As soon as everyone is frantically trying to close their positions in my stock quickly, then I sell too.

Profit Taking

If you have a long position and the price goes into profit, then you can protect your profit by:

Best selling

Sell when a closing price is below an opening.

Sell when the price falls after the opening by half the average range.

Set the stop below the previous day's low.

Sell when the price closes below the two previous closing prices and below the opening.

Sell at the third strong positive bar of the next smaller time frame. For example, if the price breaks into the profit zone on the weekly chart, then you sell after the third consecutive day in a row.

Anticipation

The following factors are important in anticipating the completion of a pattern or reversal. You can build parts of a position at an early stage before all criteria are met. Remember: The stated goal is to make profitable trading and not to be in the market at 90% of all price moves. Learn to settle for small pieces of the market. Either you secure your profits by means of a best-order, or you sell at the first sign that the supply exceeds the demand.

The seven possible times to anticipate a pattern are:

The closing price of the bar, if a short spread indicates a low supply or low demand.

An opening course in the direction of completing the pattern.

An outbreak after opening in the direction of completing the pattern.

An outbreak after 30 minutes towards the completion of the pattern.

The course is midway through the opening and in the direction of completing the pattern.

At the closing price if the pattern is fully developed.

For a correction movement after completing the pattern.

For many patterns, it can be seen that the price will fall back into the buy

zone, but the pattern will be completed above the buy zone. Then it has to be decided on a case-by-case basis which measure is the right one.

The Time-Break-Out Rule

A common approach is to trade the breakout from the first 30-minute bar, with the stop loss at the other end of this bar. This approach has been tested using S & P's market data over 14 years. Trading according to this rule leads to huge losses. It should be noted that this method has been profitable in recent years. But one must always keep in mind the fact that how dangerous it can be, if too short a test period is chosen to check a method. When entering a position, the 30-minute rule may be useful, but as with most tools, isolated use will not work.

Price Gaps

Normally, a positive price gap is considered a sign of strength and a buy signal. In verifying this assumption, it turned out that the exact opposite is true. The review was based on two methods:

Sale with a positive price gap.

Sale on a positive price gap, but only if the price falls back to the previous day high.

For purchases, the opposite applies. Both approaches were tested by computer without stops and as day trades. The second approach turned out to be almost twice as successful as the first. It is used approximately 60 times a year per future. The course must go in your direction before doing anything. This signal provides a clear market advantage, but in most cases does not make up for the fees and slippage.

But when combined with other filters and more meaningful stop management, this is a valuable addition to your trading arsenal. Coincidentally, the review found that this could be a profitable trading system for bonds.

This pattern is very similar to a pattern developed by Larry Williams called Oops. The starting point is the same, but we do not know which entry and exit criteria were used by him. The information can be reused as follows:

The signal is likely to be more reliable if the price has already gone one way and the expected end of that price movement is within range. Then this could be a good way to realize profits and perhaps build up counter positions.

Other ideas are:

Watch out for introductory signals on reverse movements of the last closing price, several previous closing prices, and several previous highs and lows.

Consider setting a half-span stop after boarding.

Watch price gaps above or below a cluster of close closing prices.

Look for a reversal after half the gap in the price gap before opening a position.

These simple computer tests will tell you quickly whether such an opening with a price gap will give you a technical advantage in view of past price developments or not. Larry Williams and Toby Crabel have made a name for themselves in this field. Whole volumes could be filled solely with the study of price movements in relation to the opening and the movement away from the opening price.

Chapter 6. Options Pricing

Options traders need to comprehend extra factors that influence an option's price and the complexity of picking the right technique. When a stockbroker becomes acceptable at foreseeing the future price movement, the person may believe it is a simple change from options, but this isn't accurate. Options traders must deal with 3 shifting parameters that influencethe price: the underlying time, volatility, and security. Changes in any of these factors affect the option's value.

Option pricing hypothesis utilizes factors (exercise price, stock price, interest rate, time to expiration, volatility) to value an option hypothetically. It estimates an option's reasonable value, which traders join into their techniques to maximize profits. Some ordinarily utilized models to value options are Black-Scholes, Monte-Carlo, and Binomial Option Pricing.

These speculations have wide margins for error because of deriving their values from different assets, typically the cost of an organization's basic stock. There are scientific formulas intended to compute the fair, reasonable value of an option. The broker inputs known factors and finds a solution that depicts what the option should be worth.

The essential objective of any option pricing model is to compute the probability that an option will be worked out or be in-the-money (ITM) at lapse. Basic asset value (stock value), interest rate, exercise price, time to expiration, and volatility, which is the number of days between the computation date and the option's exercise date, are usually utilized variables that are input into logical models to derive an option's hypothetical fair value.

Here are the general impacts that factors have on an option's cost:

Strike Price and Underlying Price

The value of puts and cuts are influenced by changes in the fundamental stock cost in a generally clear manner. When the stock cost goes up, calls should gain value since you can purchase the underlying asset at a lower cost than where the market is, and puts should diminish. In like manner, put options should increase in value, and calls should drop as the stock value falls, as the put holder gives the right to sell stock at costs over the falling market cost.

That pre-determined price to purchase or sell is known as the option's exercise price or strike price. Suppose the strike price permits you to purchase or sell the basic at a level that allows for a quick profits purchase, discarding that exchange in the open market. In that case, the option is in- the-money (for instance, a call to purchase shares at $10 when the market cost is currently $15, you can make a prompt $5 profit).

Like most other monetary resources, options costs are affected by prevailing interest rates and are affected by interest rate changes. Put option and call option premiums are affected contrarily as interest rates change lose value while calls benefit from rising rates. The inverse is genuine when interest rates fall.

The impact of volatility on an option's price is the most difficult concept for beginners to comprehend. It depends on a measure called statistical (also known as historical) volatility, SV for short, looking at past value developments of the stock over a given timeframe.

Option pricing models necessitate the trader to go in future volatility throughout the life of the option. Normally, options traders don't generally know what it will be and need to guess by working the pricing model "in reverse." The merchant knows the cost at which the option is trading and can inspect different factors, including dividends, interest rates, and time left with a bit of research. Subsequently, the main missing number will be future volatility, which can be evaluated from different information sources.

Factors That Affect an Option's Price

You cannot price an option until you realize what makes up its worth. An options trade can turn into a mind-boggling machine of legs, numerous orders, Greeks, and adjustments. However, if you don't have the foggiest idea about the essentials, what are you attempting to achieve?

When you take a look at an option chain, have you considered how they generated every one of those prices for the options? However, these options are not created randomly but rather calculated out utilizing a model, for example, the Black-Scholes Model. We will dive further into the Black- Scholes Model's seven components and how and why they are utilized to determine an option's cost/price. Like all models, the

Black-Scholes Model has a shortcoming and is a long way from perfect.

History of the Black-Scholes Model

The Black-Scholes Model was distributed in 1973 as The Pricing of Options and Corporate Liabilities in the Journal of Political Economy. It was created by Myron Scholes and Fisher Black as an approach to evaluate the price of an option after some time. Robert Merton later distributed a subsequent paper, further extending the comprehension of the model. As with any model, a few assumptions must be comprehended.

The rate of profit for the riskless asset is constant.

The more the option will be worth, the underlying follows, which expresses that move in an unpredictable and random path.

There is no riskless profit, arbitrage, opportunity.

It is possible to lend and borrow any amount of money at a riskless rate.

It is possible to purchase or short any amount of stock. There are no charges or costs.

The model has seven factors: strike price, stock price, interest rates, types of
option, dividends, time of expiration, and future volatility.

Stock Price

If a call option permits you to purchase a stock at a pre-determined cost later on, then the higher that cost goes, the more the option will be worth.

Which option would have a higher worth:

A call option permits you to purchase TOP (The Option Prophet) for $100 while it is trading at $80 or

A call option will enable you to buy TOP for $100 while it istrading at $120

Nobody will pay $100 for something they can purchase on the open marketfor $80, so our option in Choice 1 will have a low worth.

All the more alluring is Choice 2, an option to purchase TOP for $100 when it's worth is $120. In this circumstance, our option worth will be higher.

Strike Price

The strike price follows the same lines as the stock price. At the point whenwe group strikes, we do it as in-the-money, at-the-money, or out-of-the- money. When a call option is in-the-money, it implies the stock price/cost is higher than the strike cost. The stock price is not exactly the strike price when a call is out-of-the-money.

A TOP call has a strike of fifty while TOP is presently trading at $60. This option is in-the-money.

The stock price is not exactly the strike price when a put option is in the money. A put option is out-of-the-money when the stock price is greater than the strike price.

A TOP put has a strike of twenty while TOP is presently trading at $40. This option is out-of-the-money.

In-the-money options have a greater value contrasted with out-of-the-money options.

Type of Option

This is likely the easiest factor to comprehend. An option is either a call or a put, and the option's estimation will change appropriately.

A call option gives the holder the option or right to purchase the basic at a predefined cost within a particular timeframe.

A put option gives the holder the option or right to sell the hidden at a predefined price within a particular timeframe.

If you are long a call or short a put, your option value increments as the market moves higher. Suppose you are short a call or long a put your option value increments as the market go lower.

Time to expiration

Options have a constrained life expectancy; thus, their worth is influenced by the progression of time. As the time to expiration upturns, the value of the option increments. As the time to termination draws nearer, the value of the option starts to diminish. The value starts to quickly diminish within the last 30 days of an option's life. The additional time an option has till termination/expiration, the option needs to move around.

Interest Rates

The interest rate has a nominal effect on an option's value. When interest rates rise, a call option's value will rise, and a put option's value will decrease.

To drive this idea home, how about we take a look at the dynamic procedure of investing in TOP while trading at $50.

We can purchase 100 shares of the stock altogether, which would cost us $5,000.

Instead of purchasing the stock altogether, we can get long an at-the-money call for $5.00. Our all-out expense here would be $500. Our underlying cost of money would be littler, and this would leave us $4,500 leftover. Also, we will have a similar prize potential for half the risk. Presently we can take that additional money and invest it somewhere else, for example, through Treasury Bills. This would create a guaranteed return on our investment in TOP.

The higher the interest rate, the more appealing the subsequent option becomes. In this manner, when interest rates go up, calls are a superior investment, so their cost likewise increments.

On the other side of that coin, if we look at a long put versus a long call, we can see an impediment. We have two options when we want to play an underlying drawback.

You can short a hundred shares of the stock that would produce money for the business and earn interest in that money.

You long a put which will cost you less money by and large but notput additional money into your business that produces interest income.

The higher the interest rate, the more appealing the primary option becomes. Accordingly, when interest rates rise, the value of put optionsdecreases.

Dividends

Options don't get dividends, so their value varies when profits are discharged. When an organization discharges dividends, they have an ex-dividend date. If you own the stock on that date, you will be granted the dividend. Additionally, on this date, the estimation of the stock will diminish by the number of dividends. As dividends increment, a put option's value likewise increments, and a calls' value declines.

Volatility

Volatility is the main evaluated factor in this model. The volatility that is utilized is forward. Forward volatility is the proportion of implied volatility over a period later on.

Implied volatility shows the "simplified" development in a stock's future volatility. It discloses to you how traders think the stock will move. Implied volatility is constantly communicated as a percentage, non-directional, and on a yearly premise.

Chapter 7. Tips and Tricks in Stocks

This is a much better and more successful strategy. Here are some helpful tips and tricks that should guide you as you trade online in options.

The Price of Any Stock Can Move in 3 Basic Directions

These directions are up, down, and no movement at all. Depending on the kind of call that you have, you can leverage this movement to make a profit or at least avoid incurring losses.

Plenty of first-time traders and investors assume that prices of securities will go either up or down. However, this is the wrong school of thought because sometimes there is no movement at all in the price of stocks and shares. This is a very important fact in the world of options trading.

There are plenty of real-life, practical examples that show a particular stock or share which did not move significantly for quite a lengthy period. For instance, the KOL share traded within a $4 range for a total of

23 days. If you had invested money in either a call option or a put option through this stock, you would have lost money.

A purchase of a call option is usually with the hope that prices will go up. In the event that prices do rise, then you will make a profit. At other times, the prices will remain the same or even fall. In such events, if you have an out-of-the-money call, the option will most likely expire, and you will lose your investment. In the event that the price remains stagnant and you have an in-the-money option, then you will at least recoup some of the money you invested.

There will be sometimes when frustrations engulf you. This is when you just sit and watch prices start to skyrocket just a couple of weeks after the options you purchased had expired. This is often an indicator that your strategy was not on point and you did not give it sufficient time. Even seasoned traders sometimes buy call options that eventually expire in a given month and then the stock prices rise sharply in the following month.

It is therefore advisable to purchase a longer-term call option rather than one that expires after a single month. Now, since stocks move in 3 general directions, it is assumed that close to 70% of options, traders with long call and put options suffer losses. On the other hand, this implies that 70% of options sellers make money. This is one of the main reasons why conservative options traders prefer to write or sell options.

Before Buying a Call or Put Option, Look at the Underlying Stock's Chart

Basically, you want to find out as much information as possible about the performance and worth of an underlying stock before investing in it.

You should, therefore, ensure that you take a serious look at the chart of the stock. This chart should indicate the performance of the stock in the last couple of days. The best is to look at a stock's performance in the last 30 and 90 days. You should also take a look at its last year's performance.

When you look at the charts, look at the movement of the shares and try and note any trends. Also, try and observe any general movement of the shares. To identify the trend of a particular stock, try and draw a straight line along in the middle of the share prices. Then draw a line both above and below so as to indicate a channel of the general flow of the share.

Chart Readings and Buying Call Options

Let us assume that you wish to invest in a call option. Then you should ask yourself if the stock price is likely to rise and why. If you think that the stock will rise and trade at a higher level, then you may be mistaken, unless something drastic happens or new information becomes evident. New information can be a shareholders' meeting, impending earnings announcement, a new CEO, product launch, and so on.

If there is a chart showing the presence of support at lower prices and stock prices fall to that level, then it may be advisable to buy call options. The call option will be a great bet when prices are down because prices will very likely head back up. However, never allow greed to occupy your mind. When you see a profit, take and do not wait too long.

Chart Readings and Buying Put Options

Now, supposing the stock chart indicates a solid resistance at a higher price. If the stock is beginning to approach this higher level, then it is possible that the price might begin to move in that direction as well. So as the price moves, expect to gain small but significant profits. Avoid greed, so anytime the stock price falls, simply move in and make some money.

Chart Readings for Purchase of Call and Put Options

Now, if your chart readings indicate that the shares are within the lower levels of their range, then it is likely that daily changes in price will send it towards the middle of the range. If this is so, then you should move in and make a profit as soon as the price tends upwards. Even minor profits such as buying at $1 and selling at $1.15 mean a 15% profit margin.

Find Out the Breakeven Point Before Buying Your Options

Now, you need to identify a call option that you wish to invest in, especially after studying its performance on the market. Before buying, however, you should work out the breakeven point. In order to find this breakeven point, you will have to consider things such as the commissions charged and the bid spread.

It is very important that you are positive that the underlying stock of your options will move sufficiently so as to surpass the breakeven point and earn a tidy profit. You should, therefore, learn how to work out the breakeven point in an options trade.

Calculating the Breakeven Point

As an options trader, you need to know how to calculate and find the breakeven point. In options trading, there are basically 2 break-even points. With short-term options, you need to make use of the commission rates and bid spread to work out the breakeven point. This is if you intend to hold on to the options until their expiration date.

Now, if you are seeking short-term trade without holding on to the options, then find out the difference between the asking price and bid price. This difference is also known as the spread.

If You Are Dealing with Call and Put Options, Embrace the Underlying Stock's Trend

As an investor and trader in options, you need to consider the trend of the underlying stock as your friend. This means that you should not fight it. Basically, if the stock price is headed upwards, you should find a strategy that is in tandem with this movement. If you oppose it, you are unlikely to win.

Similarly, if the stock is on a downward trend, then do not oppose this movement but try and find a strategy that will accommodate this trend. You need to understand, however, that this saying is intended to guide you but is not necessarily a rule. This means that you apply it even while you consider all other factors. For instance, the major news may have an immediate effect on the price trend of a stock or shares.

As a trader, you should learn to jump successfully on a trend and follow the crowds rather than go to extremes and oppose it.

When Trading Options, Watch Out for Earnings Release Dates

Call and put options are generally expensive with the price increases significantly if there is an earnings release announcement looming. The reason is that the anticipation of very good or very bad earnings reports will likely affect the stock price. When this is an underlying stock in an options trade, then you should adjust your trades appropriately.

As an example, stocks such as Google may rise insanely during the earningsannouncement week only to dip significantly shortly thereafter. Consider Apple shares that were trading at $450 at the markets. Call options with Apple as the underlying stock were trading at $460. However, the market had targeted a price of $480 within 3 days, which did not happen. This cost investors' money. Such underlying assets are considered volatile due to the high increase in price, rapid drop shortly thereafter and related risk of losingmoney.

Chapter 8. How to Double or Triple Your Returns

You are the one responsible for turning your venture into foreign exchange into a successful endeavor. That is one of the great things about the stock. You do not have a boss screaming down your neck, telling you to do something you do not agree with. You can come up with your trading plan based on your own research and your knowledge. That being said, success can come more quickly for some than for others, and a lot of the time, this has to do with approaching this endeavor with the right strategy. We will provide you with three strategies designed to help you make this stock as profitable as possible (with as little loss as possible).

Buy Low and Sell High

If you began stock trading today with $25,000 in your pocket and access to a trading platform, all ready and raring to go, how would you know what is low and what is high? It's your first day. Naturally, for you to understand what would represent a good low investment and conversely what is high, you need to know the exchange rate history of that currency. Maybe the exchange rate for the Japanese yen seems low, but actually, compared to last year or a few months ago, it's a little high. Now it would not be a good time to buy.

Maybe the pound seems low right now, but yesterday the British government announced that the first round of the Brexit negotiations with the EU failed, and therefore, the pound may have room to go lower than it is when you logged onto your trading platform. You can wait and see what the pound is today or tomorrow and buy then.

The point here is that buying low and selling high requires understanding the patterns associated with that stock and what might cause it to go up or down. And that's merely the buying side of things. Once you have bought low, you need to figure out when you are going to sell. This is where a good trading plan will come into play. A good plan will prevent you from sellingtoo soon, or even not selling soon enough.

Focus on Not Losing Money Rather Than on Making Money

This may not be an easy strategy to understand initially, in part because notlosing money and making money seem like two sides of the same coin.

They are, but they are not identical. One of the personality types that is associated with difficulty in finding success in trading is the impulsive type. This type of person wants to make money and they want to make it quick.

They have a vague strategy about how they plan on doing that, but the mostimportant thing to them is that they have a high account balance to make as many trades as they need to turn a profit. This is the wrong approach.

Currencies are not the same as stocks. A stock's value may change very little even over a week, so the strategy that involves a lot of trades to make money is usually not the best strategy. You need a clear idea of when you are going to but, yes, because you want to make money, but mostly because you don't want to lose.

Every market that involves exchanges, like the stock market, has some implicit risk, and stock trading is risky, too, because you may be tempted to give up the advantage you have to try and make money quickly.

Develop a Sense of Sentiment Analysis

All right, the third strategy was going to be about Fibonacci retracement, which is a type of technical analysis of the market, but as this is the basics of stock trading, we are going to go into a different strategy that is not any easier than a Fibonacci retracement, just different. Sentiment analysis is a term that is used in many different specialties, not just finance, and it is not easy to describe.

It is essentially a type of analysis that is not based on a chart showing exchange rates over time (technical analysis) or understanding a factor that might today be affecting the value of the stock (fundamental analysis).

Sentiment analysis attempts to gauge the tone of the market, the direction the market is heading in, by parsing all of the available information.

A key to understanding sentiment analysis is likening it to public opinion. The economy may be booming, people have more money in their pocket, so this hypothetical country's stock should increase in value, but maybe it doesn't. Maybe there is something that is causing the market to be bearish, which might cause the stock to drop.

As you perhaps can tell, as this analysis is not based on any concrete information, it can be thought of as intuitive and no one has intuition on day 1. Let's be honest about that. Intuition comes from experience. But the purpose of this strategy is to introduce to you the idea that not the foreign exchange market, like any market, is not going to behave like a machine because it's not a machine.

Markets are places where human beings come together and humans are unpredictable, often in a frustrating way. Perhaps one day, stock trading may be handled by machines (that wouldn't be fun), but that day is far off and so you will have to develop your own sense of where the market seems to be going and use this as a strategy to achieve success in this endeavor.

Regardless of the investment that you make, be sure always to do your research. Doing research is a must. It is what will increase your chances of making the right investment decision.

The more that you understand something, the more likely it that you will be able to predict how it will move in the market. This is why doing research is essential. It will allow you to know if something is worth investing in or not. Remember that you are dealing with a continuously moving market, so it is only right that you keep yourself updated with the latest developments and changes. The way to do this is by doing research.

Whether you will start forex trading or trade in general, it is always good to have a plan. Make sure to set a clear direction for yourself. This is also an excellent way to avoid being controlled by your emotions or becoming greedy. You should have a short-term plan and a long-term plan. You should also be ready for any form of contingency.

Make your plans practical and reasonable. Remember that you ought to stick to whatever project you come up with, so be sure to keep your ideas real. Before you come up with an idea, you must first have quality information. Again, this is why doing research is very important.

What if you fail to execute your plan? This is not uncommon. If this happens to you, relax and think about what made you fail to stick to your plan? Was it favorable to you or not? Take some time to analyze the situation and learn as much as you can from it. Indeed, having a plan is different from executing it. It is more challenging to implement a plan as it demands that you take positive actions.

Learn from Your Competitors

Pay attention to your competitors and learn from them. Studying your competitors is also an excellent way to identify your strengths and weaknesses. You can learn a great deal from your competitors, especially ideas on how you can better improve your business.

Your competitors can also help you promote your trading goals and draw more techniques. This way, you get a better idea of how to trade. You do not have to fight against your competitors; you can work together.

It is prevalent for people online to support one another. , it is a good practice that you connect with other traders, especially those who are in the same niche. Do not think of them as your direct competitors, and you might be surprised just how friendly they can be.

Now, a common mistake is to consider yourself always better than others. This is wrong as you are only deluding yourself, making you fail to see the bigger picture. Instead of still seeing yourself as better than your competitors, learn from them, and see how you can use this knowledge to improve your trading endeavors.

Cash-Out

Some people who trade forex or invest in cryptocurrency commit the mistake of not making a withdrawal. The reason why they do not cash out is so that they can grow their funds. Since you can only earn a percentage of what you are trading/investing, having more funds in your account means making a higher profit return. Although this may seem reasonable, it is not a recommended approach. It is strongly advised that you should request a withdrawal. You should understand that the only way to enjoy your profits is by turning them into cash; otherwise, it is only as if you were using a demo account. Also, by making a withdrawal, you lower your risks since the funds you withdraw will no longer be exposed to risks.

You do not have to remove all your profits right away. If you want, you can withdraw 30% of your total profits, allowing the remaining 70% to add up to the funds in your account. The important thing is to make a withdrawal still now and then.

Take a Break and Have Fun

Making money online can be exciting and fun but it can also be a tiring journey. Therefore, give yourself a chance to take a break from time to time. When you take a break, do not spend that time thinking about your online business. Instead, you should spend it to relax your body and clear your mind. You will be more able to function more effectively if you do this.

This is an excellent time to go on a vacation with your family or friends or at least enjoy a movie night at home. Do something fun that will put your mind off of business for a while. Do not worry; after this short break, and you are expected to work even more.

Making money online is a long journey, so enjoy it. Making money onlinecan be lots of fun. Do not just connect with people to build a good following, but also try to make friends with your connections. You do not have to take things too seriously. Keep it fun and exciting.

Chapter 9. How to Become a Millionaire with Option Trading

Most investors and traders at the securities markets often aim to buy low then sell high and make a profit. However, options traders are the key layers in any market. This is because they can earn large amounts of money regardless of market conditions.

The options traders can make money in any market environment, even where there are no trades up or down. The reason is that options contracts are flexible in different ways. This versatility is what makes them such powerful market tools for continued profitability. Here are some profitable approaches that you can adopt to become a millionaire with option trading

Writing Options

One of the best ways of winning at options is to write options. You can write some pretty sophisticated strategies which are capable of earning your top dollars.

As a writer, you get to earn what is known as a premium. This is money that you earn even if the investor does not eventually use it. It is possible to write profitable commodities-based options regularly. Speculators can come up with profitable options that they believe will fare well in the options markets.

The Straddle Strategy

This is another approach that can help you get rich with options trading. Options mostly involve the buying of security that then turns profitable when the underlying commodity moves in a particular direction. It could be up or down but all that is necessary is a movement. A straddle is a great choice of options investment vehicle because it does not desire a specific outcome as is the case in other situations.

With a straddle, you can purchase both calls and put options with the same expiry dates and at similar strike times. The straddle strategy can be successful if and only if the underlying security of the option sees movement in either direction just so long as the movement is sufficiently large to cover the cost of premiums in both directions. Speculators can write straddle options if they believe that it is going to do well in the market.

The Collar Strategy

We also have a strategy known as the collar strategy. It is considered a pretty challenging options strategy to understand. However, a seasoned speculator can write one for you but only if he owns the underlying asset. By owning the asset, he can take the risk.

In this instance, the best option is an out-of-the-money put option. This is beneficial because should the commodity price go down, then the losses will only be minimal as it is a put option. However, should the commodity move upwards, then the trader will make a tidy profit.

The Strangle Strategy

The strangle strategy is in some ways similar to the straddle. This is because they both include the buying of a call and put option as well as the same expiration date. The only difference is that they have different strike prices. For speculators, it is possible to use the information available to enter a low-cost position.

When a trader or speculator opts for this strategy, they choose a low-cost entry because either or both of the options contracts may be bought out-of-the-money. As such, it may not be worthwhile exercising the right afforded by the shares. Both the straddle and strangle can be written by a speculator or even the trader.

So, what is the Most Profitable Options Strategy?

We have now looked at several options trading strategies, all of which are profitable and easy to execute. There are more than 40 different variations of options trading techniques. This makes it a pretty difficult job to determine the most profitable options trading strategy.

A lot of the time, traders try to find trades that will not lose their money. Also, there is a lot of varied opinions out there about the best and most profitable strategies. Fortunately, most options trading strategies offer very attractive returns with huge margins being quite common. However, it can be a risky venture, so it is advisable to proceed with caution even as you seek to become a wealthy millionaire.

Options Trading is Quite Profitable

Some express concern about profitability as well as risks posed by options trading. Fortunately, it has been proven, over the years, to be quite profitable.

Trade-in options provide you with leverage which offers you the inherent right to control a huge number of shares. This kind of leverage offers returns far greater than what selling stocks only can offer.

If you can make use of the leverage afforded by stock options, then you stand a great chance of making huge profits. These are profits made from just minuscule movements of the underlying stocks. By identifying the right strategies, then you will be able to make money regardless of the prevailing market conditions.

This means making profits even when there is no movement in the market. However, with some strategies, you may lose money if you make a wrong move. Therefore, sufficient care needs to be taken to mitigate any such losses as they can be significant.

The Most Profitable Options Trading Strategy

It is advisable, to begin with, the most basic options trading strategies first. This is the way most options traders start. By using these simple options trading strategies, you stand to make huge returns on your investments and trading skills. It is very possible to enjoy a 100% return on investment within a couple of days and sometimes even in just a couple of hours.

You can also find plenty of websites and advisory services that provide advisory services and trading assistance to traders. Some trades may fail. But it is also likely that most of your trades will be successful. Therefore, a good strategy, or approach to this challenge would be to ensure you place multiple trades on each occasion. Ensure that your strategy will win you money even though one or two trades may lose some money.

What you need to do to achieve this level of success is to work hard on your technical analysis skills. With excellent analysis skills, you will be able to analyze trades and be able to accurately determine which ones are winners and which ones you should possibly avoid. Therefore, learn to use your technical analysis tools and skills and then put them to practice often. It is only with deep knowledge of technical analysis and lots of practice that you will then be able to hone your skills and become and wealthy and successful options trader.

Consistently Profitable Strategies – Selling Puts & CreditSpreads

There are some studies conducted by credible institutions that the two most profitable options trading strategies are selling credit spreads and selling put options. The study found that the profits from such trades are consistent and regular over a long period.

However, the study found something else. The study reveals that buying call options and put options is more profitable in the long run even though it is not as consistent. You stand to make 7%-12% per month on the total portfolio which is about 84% to over 144% per annum. Considering that the techniques used are very simple, easy to apply, and require the most basic of technical analysis, then your chances of making stress-free money are very high. You can expect to win over 80% of your trades if you come up with the right trading plan.

Overall Best Options Trading Strategy

According to finds, it is widely accepted that you will make the most profits selling puts. If you invested a lot of your trading resources into selling put options, then you stand to make a lot of money consistently and with very little risk of loss.

The only challenge with the selling option is that it has certain limitations. This is because selling put options works best in a market that trends upwards or is on the rise. You can complement selling puts with selling ITM puts for long-term contracts. These are contracts that last 6 months or longer. They will make you tons of money simply because of the effect of time decay.

Also, when you sell, as a trader on the options market, credit spreads, you will be able to take advantage of the market in both directions. This means you will profit from an upward as well as downward market trend. This is great as even smaller traders can make some money regardless of experience. Therefore, always remember not to search for the size of the profits. When searching for the most profitable and successful options strategy, focus on factors like;

Ability to come up with a reliable and safe plan Have a plan that generates regular income Associated risks are low

Technical requirements are manageable

Selling Naked Puts is one of the most lucrative ways of making money trading options. The return on margin is almost as lucrative as selling credit spreads. However, it does not carry a similar level of risk. In short, anytime that you sell a put option, then you make it possible to purchase a stock at a price of your choosing.

A Closer Look at Naked Puts

It's the end of June and XYZ stock is at $50. However, the market is fluctuating and you prefer to buy this stock for $45. What you need to do at this stage is to sell a $45 put option for $2. You can put the expiration date on this option as the third week of July. Once you post the option, you will immediately receive $200 into your trading account. Now should the XYZ stock price fall below $45, you will be required to purchase 100 units. This will cost you $4,500.

However, you already have $200 in your account so the cost of buying the shares is reduced by this amount. If you sell a put option each month for the following six months, you will receive a total of $1,200. This will drastically lower the cost of buying XYZ shares. However, if the stock starts rising, you will not need to buy it but will keep selling the put option. While there is a slight risk due to liquidity issues, this strategy is quite a winner and can lead you to immense profits in just a short while.

ROI or Return on Investment

The Term ROI stands for Return on Investment. ROI is a measure of performance and is used by both investors and traders to measure the effectiveness and efficiency of an investment. This includes your trading capital. ROI deliberately endeavors to measure directly the total return derived from a particular investment.

For instance, if you invest a total of X amount on a particular trade and then received a return of Y from this investment, then ROI will endeavor to indicate the performance of your investment amount and what you received for your efforts. If you want to calculate the rate of return of an investment, you will need to know the total return which is then divided by the investment amount.

One of the most important aspects of your investment portfolio is its profitability. You need to regularly monitor your investments which are best achieved using the ROI or return on investment. It is advisable to work out what each dollar invested has generated.

R.O.I = (Profits — Costs) / Costs

Even then, investors need to understand that the ROI depends on numerous other factors such as the kind of investment security preferred and so on.

Also, note that a high ROI implies a higher risk while a lower means reduced risk. For this reason, appropriate risk management must be undertaken.

Chapter 10. How COVID-19 Will Affect Option Trading

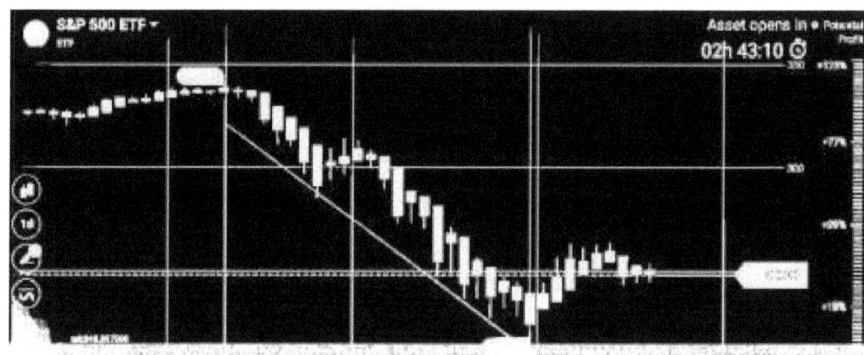

Coronavirus has had a variety of effects on global financial markets. It's difficult to say to what extent the epidemic affected people now that it's not over; between February 19 and March 23, the S & P 500 lost more than a third of its value. Over the same time frame, the Dow Jones Industrial Average has lost even more (up to 36 percent). Despite the return to growth, both indicators point to a massive disruption in the global economy that hasn't been seen in the last five years. Furthermore, the economic effects of the world's most recent pandemic may not be limited to that. It's likely that there are already undiscovered or delayed effects that will be found later.

Despite the recent recovery, the economic downturn in China, the United States, and Europe still have the potential to cause a full-fledged financial crisis. The current year's global GDP is very likely to experience a setback.

What should we expect?

The 'Fast Recovery' scenario, according to Roland Berger, an independent European consulting firm, is already out of the question. Their experts also predict that the outage will last between 4 and 12 weeks. China has moved further down the coronavirus curve, and its economy has regained its foothold (at least, according to the Chinese government itself). COVID-19's results, on the other hand, are still unknown in Europe and the United States. It might take a lot of time for them to recover.

Certain sectors will be affected harder than the overall economy. Airlines, leisure, and retail (with the exception of FMCG) will be hit hard. The automobile, logistics, and oil/gas industries are all in the same boat.

Financial services, on the other hand, would be significantly less impacted. Nonetheless, the pandemic's impacts would be felt to some degree by all sectors. It will definitely take some time for the global economy to recover.

The COVID-19 stay-at-home requirement has spawned a major sub- industry of options trading, which is increasing in tandem with a rise in equities trading that shows no signs of slowing down.

In November, stock options trading reached new highs, continuing a pattern that started earlier in the year.

On all options markets, equity options trading is up 50% year to date compared to last year.

Optional Equity (Volume)

- NASDAQ has a 49 percent market cap.
- CBOE has a 51% market share.
- ICE has a 58 percent share of the market.

"As you can see from the volumes, the public is accepting alternatives in a completely unparalleled manner," Interactive Brokers' Steve Sosnick told me. "I think the lockdown led to some of the popularity... Many people were stranded at home, with $1,200 checks or rent/loan moratoria, with no sports to watch or wager on. So, they went to the stock market, where they discovered that options have payout mechanisms that are identical to sportsbets."

The comparison to sports betting is intentional: "The psychology [of sports betting versus stock betting] is quite close." "With sports betting, I have a chance to win a portion of the money. It's the same with stocks and options, only there are thousands of bets you can make every day with stocks and options, and when you're in an upmarket like we have been, you can start to believe that the odds are really in your favor."

Most of the trading activity has happened in out-of-the-money options that are nearing expiration, with most of it day trading: purchasing in the morning and selling in the afternoon, according to Kyle Robinson, who monitors trading activity at Piper Sandler.

What makes you want to do that? "They're selling options because a lot of people don't have enough money to buy a lot of stocks," he said. "You can purchase options for a fraction of the price, and if your options move at the same percentage as the underlying stock, you can profit as if you owned it."

Many day traders are right to aim options trading, according to Sosnick, and are not behaving irrationally.

He pointed out that buying out of the money calls has low initial investment, so you can only lose what you put in. "You will only lose a dollar if you buy a call for a dollar." "They might be poorly capitalized," Sosnick hypothesized when asked why so many people are doing basic daytrading, in the morning and out by the close. They might crave the opportunity to sleep at night. It's possible that it's their only option."

Zero commissions on many trades, as well as the presence of social media and chat rooms full of debates on high-profile names, are all contributing to the day trading phenomenon.

Another important aspect is the availability of instructional materials that instruct traders about how to trade options.

"We have seen no decline in interest in educational content on our website," says JJ Kinahan, TD Ameritrade's Chief Market Strategist. "Stock fundamentals and getting started with options are the two most popular videos on our site." He pointed out that viewing of that content is already three times higher than a year ago.

Equity Trading is Also on the Rise

The rise in options trading is being accompanied by a similar rise in stock trading. For example, trading volume at Fidelity increased by 97 percent year over year in the third quarter.

According to Rich Repetto of Piper Sandler, regular average revenue trades (DARTs) at Interactive Brokers increased by 174 percent in November compared to the same time last year. They have added 29,000 new accounts to their scheme.

In a recent note to clients, Repetto wrote, "We are raising our 4Q20 EPS forecast due to better-than-expected trading, continued account expansion, and good margin balance and customer equity growth."

Robinson noted that trading in futures contracts, which are more often used by practitioners as hedging vehicles, and index options have not seen the same drastic rise.

How long will this high level of trading last?

What could probably go wrong in the midst of all this bullish call buying? The greatest risk, according to Sosnick, is simple mean reversion: "You may get into a losing streak." "If you buy risky calls, it doesn't take much to lose money after a few days or weeks."

Sosnick also hypothesized that, regardless of market dynamics, all of this day trading might have a finite shelf life.

"I wonder how far does this has to do with the fact that many people haven't had to pay student loans in a long time and will have to do so next month," he said. "If you use the typical student loan payment of $400 to bring in the economy, and I have to start paying that back, that is money that will come out of the markets."

Robinson concurred. Robinson told me, "We don't expect these levels to last." "Those who have stayed at home will return to work once the pandemic is over. When the vaccine is released, volatility will likely decrease, making day trading more difficult."

Sosnick decided that if the large amount of call buying stopped, volatility would decrease. He pointed out that the massive amount of call buyers has inflated implied volatility, which is one of the reasons the CBOE Volatility Index (VIX) has remained trapped at the elevated 21 levels amid a major rally.

How many people will be around for the next round of corrections?

According to Sosnick, the next correction would be the ultimate test to see if these new traders hang around.

"People are knowledgeable, and they are attempting to educate themselves. A full market cycle, on the other hand, is the best education for traders, and we haven't seen one yet. Many of these traders just entered the market after March, so they haven't seen the whole cycle."

Sosnick doesn't blame the younger generation for enjoying a good time with stocks and options when they can: "And betting on NASDAQ was much more likely to pay off than betting on the Jets," he joked.

Conclusion

Thank you for making it through to the end of this book. You've now had a careful stroll through the key standards and ventures in options trading we feel are fundamental to progress as an options trader. You've figured out how the options markets function, the best trading strategies and why it's basic to pick the best possible fundamental assets for the procedures you need to utilize. You've additionally observed that great exit strategies are nearly as imperative as discovering great trades to enter, that focusing on the points of interest is basic, and that achievement is virtually inconceivable without a decent money-management plan — and the discipline to follow it.

At last, you've got lots of pages loaded with vital inquiries to consider in your search for the best online options broker. At the end of the day, it's a great opportunity to control up, plugin — and profit. You have all the data you have to appreciate 24-hour access to the options markets, fast and programmed execution of your orders and the most reduced commissions in the history of options trading. In any case, to share these advantages, you should confront the bigger individual duties that accompany coordinated access to online trading.

You should have the discipline to do your very own research, screen your own positions and monitor every one of the points of interest you may leave to your full-benefit financial firm. You can never again depend on a broker to watch your positions and call with guidance or suggestions. You are currently an autonomous administrator — and, all things considered, must be absolutely in charge of your own behavior.

You should likewise be mindful and be prepared to react to both fast moves in everyday trading designs and consistently evolving longer-term economic situations.

In case you think tolerating such difficulties and practicing such discipline is simple, think of one as a little preventative portion of the real world. An investigation — "Online Investors: Do the Slow Die First?" by Brad M. Barber and Terrance Odean, published in Economic Intuition.

CPSIA information can be obtained
at www.ICGtesting.com
Printed in the USA
BVHW011048130522
636628BV00021B/165